UP, UP, AND AWAY!
Poems from Melton Mowbray

P. Handley

ARTHUR H. STOCKWELL LTD
Torrs Park, Ilfracombe, Devon, EX34 8BA
Established 1898
www.ahstockwell.co.uk

© P. Handley, 2014
First published in Great Britain, 2014
All rights reserved.
*No part of this publication may be reproduced
or transmitted in any form or by any means,
electronic or mechanical, including photocopy,
recording, or any information storage and
retrieval system, without permission
in writing from the copyright holder.*

*British Library Cataloguing-in-Publication Data.
A catalogue record for this book is available
from the British Library.*

ISBN 978-0-7223-4463-7
*Printed in Great Britain by
Arthur H. Stockwell Ltd
Torrs Park   Ilfracombe
Devon EX34 8BA*

NEW LAWS FOR OLD

How was it that the year gone by passed so fast?
Did I go to sleep?
And how many of my New Year resolutions
Did I fail to keep?
Well, for this coming year I've made a note
Of things that I must do –
I'm going to make the world a better place
Especially for you!

First I'll abolish all income tax
I never really wanted to join!
And the only word I can get to rhyme
Is the appropriate word 'purloin'!
Next I'd make it compulsory
That all women join the Ladies' Skittles League
For a fun-filled sporty evening,
Tinged with a little intrigue.

Every little helps you know
A family cat or dog is a pet,
So why don't they qualify for 'family allowance'?
I'll get it sorted – I guess no one's thought of it yet!
To enhance Melton as a tourist attraction
I suggest a fountain in Market Square
But instead of it flowing water,
Hot coffee would encourage people there.

My generous thoughts are beginning to ebb
But in kitty there's plenty of lolly
Therefore, for a nice New Year's gesture
How about free grub in a superstore trolley?

Well, now I've put the world to rights
I'd like to make it clear,
There's just one more thing for me to do
To wish everyone a HAPPY AND HEALTHY NEW YEAR.

YESTERYEAR

Do you remember the corner shop
In every other street?
With bell on door and mat upon floor
On which to wipe one's feet.

Sugar was weighed out
Into bags of dark blue.
The same as for currants, raisins, prunes
And sultanas too.

Remember the big slab of butter
By request cut to any weight.
With two wooden pats it was moulded –
I can remember it tasted just great!

Remember the machine that sliced bacon
Into rashers of both thick and thin.
And beautiful bread, cakes and pastries
Fresh by the baker brought in.

Oh, and the smell of freshly ground coffee
The memory for ever will stay.
And of liquorice and sherbet and pear drops
And gobstoppers which lasted all day!

Vinegar was sold straight from the barrel,
And can you believe that treacle was too?
They sold Lux flakes, Robin starch and the blue bag
And Woodbine fags at a penny for two.

They sold cheese in great lumps
And tinned pineapple chunks,
Cottons, shoelaces, Pears soap for our faces,
Carbolic soap and brushes with bristles,
Even whips and tops and coloured penny whistles.

Block salt was sold, and let me explain
Soda was bought to flush down the drain,
There were wooden pegs and rope to hold washing on line
And, as you all know,
We blackleaded the grate with a tin of Zebo.

'Twas more friendly to shop back in those days
Where a chair by the counter had space
And a word and a smile from the server,
Made the shop seem a wondrous place.

With all modern packaging of cling film and cardboard
I really can't quite come to terms –
For of folks coughing and sneezing
We built up our own resistance to germs.

Now when at superstore you've filled your trolley
And in queue at the checkout you wait,
It's no good you even suggesting:
"Pay you on Friday – just bung it all on the slate . . ."

MY WISH

I'd like to say it long – I'd like to say it loud
To all good Melton people, alone or in a crowd.
I'd say it to the policeman, the vicar and the nurse,
I'd shout it to the binman, the teacher, the driver of a hearse.
I'd mouth it to the senior citizen, the mother with her kids,
To the folk on their computers, the auctioneer a-taking bids.
I'd bellow it out loud from top of church tower
(If only I had the puff!)
And I'd yodel it over the Tannoy
Till shoppers complained, "That's enough."
I'd shout it to folk on the market stalls,
To the barman serving up drinks.
Alas, as per usual – I go on much too long, methinks,
And so, I'll yell out loud and long and even give a cheer,
To wish you all, good Melton folk,
A VERY MERRY CHRISTMAS AND A HAPPY AND
HEALTHY NEW YEAR.

FRIENDSHIP

I had a little weep today
Cos your card it made me cry,
So, to live up to those kindly words
I must do my best and try!
I'm all 'chuffed up' and feeling great,
Your gesture I really do appreciate.
Now, the thought that comes into my brain
That those words for me – I return the same,
For, my friend, I consider you to be
Amongst the best of friends God granted me.

MY WORLD

I wake up in the morning
And look through my windowpane,
The lawn is frosted over
And I think it's snowed again.
Tree branches look embossed in silver
Snowdrops stand with heads hung low,
I pull my dressing gown around me
Cos the barometer shows it's minus two below.
I watch birds scratching for their breakfast
But the ground is too iced to give,
They hide in bushes whilst I feed them
Hopefully that through the WINTER they will live.

Another day has dawned
As usual I gaze out on my garden's view,
I see the tips of daffodils and tulips
Sturdily pushing their way through.
I hear birdsong late at night and early morn
A prelude to the time
When birds will mate and build their nest,
Then much pleasure will be mine.
SPRING is the season I love best,
It seems to bring the world alive,
Dependent on the sun and rain
Assisting to make the garden thrive.

It's nice to see the SUMMER sun
Come shining through my room,
And to see the shrubs and flowers,
A glory in their bloom.
I appreciate the gentle rain that falls
To wash the ground anew,
Or to feel the warmth of sun on face
And to see a sky so blue.
It makes me really grateful
For my own piece of earthly view,
And to sit outside of an evening
And watch the stars come twinkling through.

The time to gather fruit is here,
Apple, pear and plum,
Whilst for the stalwart farmers
Another year has just begun.
The days are now much shorter
Nights grow a little colder too,
Best to make the most of these nice days
Before the AUTUMN is quite through.
The colours of the leaves that fall
Are quite a glorious sight,
I'm so pleased that I live in England
And I thank God with all my might.

I'M GOING TO . . .

I'm Going To a dance tonight
And I want to look my best,
Because the fellow who is taking me
Is far above the rest.
I know he is the one for me
I only hope he feels the same,
Why he chose to be with me
I really can't explain.

I'm Going To go on holiday
With my now husband and lovely son.
I'm so very much excited
Even before the trip's begun.
We are going to glorious Devon,
To a village near the sea,
Just walking down the narrow lanes
Gives much pleasure to us three.

I'm Going To have to tell you
That some friction has crept in,
However much I put my point
I'm never going to win.
With cricket, skittles, any sport
I'm afraid I can't compete,
This leaves us feeling neglected
And, sorry to say, 'defeat'.

I'm Going To feel much happier now
Everything is going to be OK,
I've joined in playing skittles
And many women also play.
Things are so much better now
The skies seem always blue,
We'd qualify for the Dunmow flitch
Is what I'm telling you.

I'm Going To admit – there's a cloud on my horizon,
Dear husband is not at all well,
Funny how life can change so quickly
Into a living hell.
But medical skill did put him right,
To all involved, "God bless"
With luck and determination
Hubby got himself out of a mess.

I'm Going To say I'm amazed
How quickly years seem to slide,
Both now retired and happy
Exploring the countryside.
We enjoy tending to our garden
And friends we have known many years,
Together we've had much pleasure
With laughter and sometimes a few tears.

I'm Going To a funeral
With my son and his family,
To say farewell to 'My Handsome'
A sad time for all you'll agree.
Fifty-three years we were granted,
Our marriage was one of the best,
Looking around at our friends and our family
I'd say that we truly were blessed.

ROLES REVERSED

"Sonny Boy, come on now, get out of bed,
You'll be late for school – use your head!
Did you wash your neck – clean your teeth as well?
Blow your nose – you haven't cleaned your shoes as I can tell.
Have you got a hankie? Your hair looks such a mess!
Did you spend your dinner money? Come on now, confess!
Have you changed your socks? Cos they really start to smell
Some things you do make me run my soul into hell!"

"Mother – look at you – you've only walked a step or two
And you are puffing like a horse!
Keep out that ruddy garden – but there's no telling you, of course.
You shouldn't climb those steps – I'm thinking just of you,
Those plant pots that you carry are far too heavy too.
I'm calling Dr Who as that cough you've got is chronic,
He may send you to hospital or just prescribe a tonic!
Do as you are told – do I make my feelings plain?
Get to bed cos I can see that you're in pain!"

Though times have changed
It doesn't change the love I have for you,
So HAPPY BIRTHDAY, son,
May all your dreams come true!

COLOURS

R   **R**adiance portrays the colour of RED,
         'A sign of Richness' 'tis often said.

A   **A**mply blessed for both colour and fruit,
         ORANGE is a colour with no substitute.

I   **I**dentifying with sunshine and welcome spring flower,
         YELLOW gives us pleasure that never grows sour.

N   **N**othing can compare with the versatile GREEN
         Of trees, shrubs and grassland – such beauty to be seen.

B   **B**oldly representing a cloudless sky,
         BLUE is a colour giving treat to every eye.

O   **O**nly INDIGO makes us query the hue,
         Is it a purple or could it be darkest blue?

W   **W**hat a beautiful flower is the VIOLET,
         And the colour is so lovely too.
         As is each colour of the RAINBOW
         To cheer us our whole life through!

IT'LL BE ALL RIGHT ON THE NIGHT
(We Hope!)

Oft-times I go for practice
With that wonderful, versatile pair,
'She' known as Madeline 'Rogers'
'He' as 'Twinkle Toes' Ted 'Astaire'.

"Right," sez Ted, "shall we make a start?
I suggest that it's time to begin.
Enough of your gossip and chatter
Of whether you're fat or you're thin.

"Madeline, the piece you are singing is sad,
So show compassion and sorrow and grief.
The way that you're smiling and grinning
Is really beyond my belief.

"It's time that we tried a duet now
(I'm beginning to think that we've won),
But why hasn't one of you started,
Whilst the other has finished and done?

"Listen, Phyllis, to that which I tell you –
Your voice is too loud and too strong.
You sound more like a chap with a barrow,
You're supposed to be singing a song."

Now it's Ted's turn to tickle the ivories,
Of his playing he never does brag,
But heaven help those who'd but whisper
Whilst he's playing his 'Black and White Rag'.

When people ask us to perform,
It's rare that we refuse,
It gives sadistic pleasure
Folks' hearing to abuse!

"Please come," they say,
"A captive audience we assure."
Too right that they'll be 'captive'
For we'll bolt up every door.

And when we've played and sung
And given best of all we can,
We'll guarantee that sales will soar
Of Aspros, Hedex and Phyllosan.

Maybe, just maybe, sometime in the future,
Every person in the country
Will be glued to their TV,
Watching a fabulous show called *Old Faces*,
Featuring Madeline, Ted and Me . . .

ADDICTION

I get up in the morning
Make a big strong cup of tea,
Then whilst I chew my cornflakes
I switch on my TV.
There's that cheeky chappie Kilroy
Debating "Is it right or wrong,
To do one's shopping in a superstore
Dressed only in a thong?"

Next it's *City Hospital* time
Showing people sick and ill,
It's made me feel quite poorly,
I'll have to take a pill.
I really ought to go make my bed,
But I feel compelled to look,
And at eleven o'clock on BBC1,
It's *Ready, Steady, Cook*!

I'll just watch *House Invaders*
For ideas on how to decorate,
Then it's the news on Channel 5,
To keep me up to date.
Twelve thirty's time for *Doctors*
Then I **must** go make the bed,
But it's *Shortland Street* on ITV,
So I'll just watch that instead!

A cup of coffee now
And a snack of beans on toast,
Then to watch a chat show,
With Oprah Winfrey as the host.
Three o'clock it's *Keeping Up Appearances*
At the same time a feather duster I will flick,
Cos that slovenly Daisy and Onslo,
Are enough to make one sick.

Three o'clock's *Collector's Lot*
I suppose I could compete
With this massive pile of toffee papers,
Lying around my feet.
Four o'clock – *Fifteen to One*
Time to get hubby's dinner on,
Oh, just scrub and bake a spud
Then tart it up to look quite good!

Countdown's next,
With Vorderman and Whiteley.
Did I make the bed?
Crikey, not ruddy likely!
Pet Rescue's at five,
Good heavens alive . . .
I've burnt the fish fingers,
Will I survive?

Quarter past five – *The Weakest Link*
Just bung the dishes in the sink –
Six o'clock we watch the news
"Would you like a pudding – you can choose . . .
To save washing up any more plates,
Have an apple or a 'nana or some seedless grapes!"
Six thirty there's a report on the weather,
Ah! One still has to do shopping and housework – whatever . . .

"Are you all right, love? You look a bit pale . . .
Sit down and put your feet up – we'll watch *Emmerdale*."
Coronation Street is next,
That Les Battersby gets me real vexed.
University Challenge is on BBC2 at eight,
A bit of culture's never too late!
Only Fools and Horses is a good repeat
Then, *Peak Practice* keeps me off my feet.

"Put the kettle on – let's have a cuppa,
Would you like a biscuit for your supper?"
Charlie Dimmock's next on BBC2,
You know – she sure sets your eyes aglow!
You want to watch the *News at Ten*?
Don't watch that depressing stuff again –
You what? You think it's time you went to bed –
Was it something that I said?

Well, I'll be there when I've seen the film on Channel 4,
Yes, I know I've seen it twice before,
But I reckon if it's my only real chance
To really enjoy a bit of romance!
Gosh! it's midnight – I must have dozed off,
I missed the end and I feel quite cross!
The TV's on all through the night,
To watch it would not be right!

Did I wake you, dear?
You know, we pay all that money on a licence for TV,
And I think, with me you will agree
That it's nothing but a load of rubbish that we see!
Why should I pay all that hard-earned cash,
To sit around and watch such utter trash?
Bring me a cuppa when you go to work,
For to get up early I must not shirk.
I like to keep an eye on time,
Cos *Kilroy*'s on BBC1 promptly at nine!

UP, UP, AND AWAY!

On a glorious summer's evening
When the sun was still quite high,
I climbed into a basket
And floated to the sky.

The balloon that was above me
Was magnificent to behold,
Royal blue and scarlet
And a lovely splash of gold.

The higher I ascended
The more spellbound I became,
As my eyes devoured the beauty
Of the wonderful terrain.

The earth looked like a patchwork quilt
Laid on a bed king-sized,
Miles and miles of Lilliput Land
Stretched before my eyes.

Trees and houses looked so small
To me they seemed unreal,
Now I truly realise
How Gulliver did feel.

The silence was so deafening
I found it hard to think,
Apart from the hot air firing
Bringing me back to the brink.

All too soon the journey
Came gently to an end,
As slowly, very slowly,
We started to descend.

As the ground began to rise
My heart began to thump,
My wonderful dream was shattered
I came back to earth with a bump!

NAIVETY

I clearly remember, whilst still at school
My teacher said to me,
"Now tell me, child, when you leave here
What **do** you intend to be?"
I thought awhile then gave a smug smile
"That's easy," I said, "for, you see –
I'm going to be a lady,
And have everyone wait upon me!"

How Naive Can One Be?

So, came fourteen years and I left school
Lots of money all eager to make –
To buy dresses and chocolate and make-up
The very thought was my first big mistake!
"You'll do as you're told!" said my parents,
"And study hard for another two years."
And I had to do as I was bidden,
In spite of my tantrums and tears!

How Naive Can One Be?

My friends were all earning money,
In shoe factory, or Woolies, or mill,
Whilst I was still classed as a 'schoolkid'
The embarrassment made me feel quite ill.
'Ah well,' I thought, 'when I get a job
I should get a good salary . . .'
Just goes to show how wrong one can be –
The princely sum of forty bob,
Was what was paid to me!

How Naive Can One Be?

Now when I met my ideal mate,
Wed, and had a family,
I thought, 'This is it – now I can lead
A life of luxury!' Foolish person . . .
For life's all 'want', and 'want' must pay
So back to work I must –
To earn lots of necessary pennies,
For to buy the things I lust.

How Naive Can One Be?

"I'll work a year then pack it in."
But most plans go awry,
And the years they pass so quickly
You don't notice they've gone by.
But the cooker needs replacing and the washer's gone kaput,
Better get 'em sorted, because
Retirement's just afoot,
Then I'll stay at home and be an 'idle me'.

How Naive Can One Be?

Retired at last! Each day I'll get up early
To clean the whole house through,
Then to friends serve tea and sandwiches
Like a lady – as I planned to do –
Joke! I lie in bed till eight or so,
Ignore the dust and muck,
Get out barrow, fork and hoe
And into gardening I get stuck.
My hands are rough and grimy,
With nails all split and torn.
But I've never been so happy since the day that I was born.
Who'd **want** to be a lady – to entertain and serve up tea?
How Positively, Absolutely, Naive Can A Person Be?

PHONE!

Is that the phone ringing, Bill?
OK, I'll answer it, you just sit yourself still.
Hello – 95493 – Phyllis speaking – who is calling?
Oh, I see, well, no problem, there's nothing spoiling.

So, what's the weather like with you?
Cold and damp – yes, the same here too!
Where did you go for your hols this year?
No, we could only afford it to Skeggy, I fear . . .

How's your health, dear – are you keeping fit and well?
Oh, I've had my share of colds and flu, I can tell . . .
Is hubby all right? What job's he in now?
(I hope you don't think me a nosey old . . . !)

Kiddies all right – is it one, two, or three?
Yes, it takes something to keep 'em –
You're telling me!
Did you see programme on telly
'Bout kids – sex, drugs and drink?
Aye, it's a worry having youngsters,
It sure makes you think!

What about this latest rise
In banking interest rate?
It won't affect me any,
Cos I'm living off the state.
The National Health's a worry –
What happens when you're ill?
It won't be long before they cure you
By killing you with a pill!

You know, the price you have to pay
For just a loaf of bread!
We've given it up completely –
We're eating cake instead!
Gosh, my rheumatic pains
Are giving me some welly . . .
Bill, I can't hear myself think
Turn the sound down on the telly!

Hello, hello, are you still there?
There's a lot of interference
On this line I do declare.
Did I tell you I lost my pension book?
Oooh, it gave me quite a fright . . .
I couldn't sleep for worry,
I was awake for half the night.
Eventually I found it –
The subject is quite sore,
I'd tucked it in my thermals,
In my winter woollies' drawer.

I beg your pardon – oh, you think it time to go?
I've enjoyed our little chinwag –
It's bucked me up you know.
Bye-bye now, with best regards
To you and your family,
Wishing you the best of everything
From us two – Bill and me.

Right, Bill, put kettle on for cup of tea
My throat it really is quite dry,
I couldn't get a word in edgeways
As hard as I might try.
Who was that? Really, Bill,
Can't you guess? You are amazing –
It was some poor soul with the rotten job
Of selling double glazing.

MORE MELTON MEMORIES

I thought once more I'd like to try
To remember Melton in the days gone by.
And so I've tried to remember more
By dipping into my memory store:

Evacuating to Melton Mowbray at the start of World War II
As a child, seemed a most exciting thing to do.
There we lodged in a house on Snow Hill,
Opposite Palmers Shoe Factory – can you remember it still?
Snow Hill fields were a wonderful place to play,
Shouting and echoing under the bridge on the way.
Women's Land Army were billeted nearby
And we'd wave as tractor or horse and cart rolled by.

Northern Railway line ran past there to the coast,
And a well-patronised bar the station could boast.
Entry could be gained by tunnel underground
Now somewhere in that vicinity Melton Co-op can be found.
In Stanley Street, the two sisters, the Misses Barrett kept their shop,
Selling everything from soap, pegs, sweets, to bucket and mop.
Vinegar came from a tap, and treacle was sold from a barrel,
And in all the clutter for sale one could buy pieces of wearing apparel.

In Pall Mall there stood a pub called Royal Oak,
Whilst further along were rooms housing 'Sally Army' folk.
At bottom of New Street was a blacksmith – Arnell's I think,
Either side of which was Freemans the dairy,
Or Rutland Arms, for choice of a drink.
Brewards on Timber Hill sold hot faggots – just take your own bowl!
Oh! The smell and the taste did wonders for the soul!
Mr Miles had shops there as well – not one, but two –
Greengrocery or fish and chips he could provide for you.

Can you recall shop of 'Skinny' Veasey?
Just a glance at his fruit made one feel really queasy.
Also in King Street – a man with much flair
Was Mr Charlie Cole, who cut gentlemen's hair.
Payne's pram shop was on the corner of Park Lane
And not far away was a train – let me explain . . .
'Twas a model in front of 'Chippy' Dixon's shop window,
Along by Wetherill's baby clothes shop, as you may know.

Bottom of Scalford Road was the cafe of Dakins
Where visitors to and from cattle market increased weekly takings.
Did you know this town had children's homes – not one but two?
Brookfield House on Snow Hill and the Homestead of Burton Road too.
Mr Skyme and Mr Heawood were photographers of good repute,
Both their styles were different, which I don't think we can dispute.
Warners was there for printing, also selling stationery
Whilst Warners, in the Market Square, sold cakes and cups of tea.

Sharman & Ladbury and Garner's garages
Were well known in town, you'll agree.
And in Nottingham Street, Hollingshead's shop
Displayed boots and saddles for all to see.
Do you remember Barton's garage – and the little island there?
Now for Melton's townsfolk it's a major thoroughfare.
But, one thing in Melton that doesn't change, and I hope it never will,
Is the beautiful church of St Mary – may it stand there for ever and still!

SHOES

Came a ratatat-tat
And down on the mat
Dropped a letter addressed to 'Yours Truly'
Tho' I knew what it said I kept a cool head,
For I'm not one to act all unruly.

"Please come to my wedding"
It said in the note,
Which brought a tear to my eye
And a lump to my throat.
Now I'm not one to muddle,
Or even to confuse,
But the thoughts that flashed before me
Were of hats, clothes and shoes.

I prudently decided
(As of money I was short)
I would wear a suit and hat
That I had recently bought.
So all that's left for me to choose
Is a comfortable and fashionable pair of shoes.

But comfort and fashion
Don't go hand in hand,
And things didn't go exactly
The way I had planned.
There were thousands of shoes
Every style, shape and hue,
Shopping for shoes is an experience
I'm telling you!

I tried on court shoes, slingbacks and peep-toes,
I tried shoes on with laces, and buckles and bows,
I tried wedgies and flatties and six-inch high heels.
My poor feet were covered in blisters and weals.
Defying the heights of gravity
I chose fashion platforms – Silly Me!

The day of the wedding dawned clear and bright,
And the couple they looked a wonderful sight.
I TEETERED into the reception hall,
Fully knowing 'Pride Comes Before A Fall'!
And that's exactly what I did,
My beautiful saucepan gift taking flight from its lid.

How I slunk out from that hall
It embarrasses me to recall.
But it didn't quite end in doom and gloom,
For as the happy pair departed for honeymoon,
Hung on the bumper of their car,
Near the 'Just Married' sign –
Were a pair of platform shoes
That just used to be mine!

A SHOPPING SPREE

I'm sick of myself – I look a mess
I'll treat myself to new suit, or dress,
I've plenty **now**, I must admit
But wardrobe's damp,
They've shrunk – don't fit!

So . . . big fried breakfast to start the day,
Wash the pots, then I'm away,
A leisurely day to take in town
With plenty of time to look around.

They don't make clothes like they used to do,
Seem to skimp them thro' and thro',
Fashioned for the model kind,
Not us with hips and big behind.

Can't find a thing in C&A,
So coffee and scone to keep wolf at bay,
Saw a super dress in BHS –
Would have fitted, were I three sizes less.

'Tis time for lunch – it sure smells good,
All the trimmings and steak and kidney pud.
I'll cut down and only coffee take,
Well, just one slice of delicious cheesecake.

Well fortified I stroll away
To Marks and Sparks I make my way,
Colours and styles seem bright and gay
Bound to be something to make my day.

Dorothy Perkins, Richard's, and Lewis's I try
Why I bother, I know not why,
Laura Ashley, Debenhams, Co-op too
There can't be many stores that's left to do.

Don't like frills and don't like bows,
Nothing suits me, heaven knows!
Can't stand stripes that circle round,
They show up every bump, I've found.

Oh, I don't know, I'm just fed up,
I'm going to have another cup
And perhaps a wedge of cake I'll take
Before the journey home I make.

"What did you buy?"
Greeted the cry
(I felt such a stupid prat)
"Oh, just a girdle to control the fat –
And help to keep the stomach flat . . ."

Unlike fairy stories,
There's a sad end to this tale,
Cos the 'Won't Fit' syndrome
Makes me weep and wail.

I know it's eating leftovers,
That's making me so big,
So I'll do myself a favour
And buy a pot-bellied pig!

CONVERSATION WITH A SO-CALLED 'FRIEND'

I've got to talk to someone –
To tell my tale of woe,
Although my problem's obvious
– I've let my figure go . . .

There's not a soul that I can blame
The fault is all my own,
I know you've heard it all before,
But please don't sit and groan.

Now both of us know the reason
Why I've gone to seed,
It's my all-consuming passion,
Commonly known as 'Greed'.

This time last year I was so proud –
At goal I looked quite slim,
And on my dress or blouse I wore
With pride my Goal Weight Pin.

And may I say that at the time
You seemed to point the way,
To help to make me resolute
To keep the pounds at bay.

Oh yes, you helped me very much
By boosting my morale,
Now, seems to me you're full of glee
Cos I'm a 'fatty gal'.

Yet who are you to criticise?
You're not that thin, old mate,
In fact, if I were not a lady
I'd say you carried weight!

Some days you help
Some days you don't,
I wonder, do you care?
Doesn't it ever worry you
When I stand and swear?

I'm going now – this visit must end,
No longer expect me to call you my 'friend'.
You stood and you smirked
Whilst I chewed on my nails,
Oh, how I hate you –
You 'orrible SCALES!

AND AGAIN!

I thought I'd like to try again and give it another go,
To glimpse again at Melton in the days we 'oldies' used to know.
I can recall Miss Dowson selling fabrics by the yard,
General Post Office then stood opposite – if you think about it hard.
Good old Woolies flourished here for many a year,
Why it had to go, to me is still not clear!

Attenborough's chemist was at top of High Street,
And the traditional carafes of coloured water in the window looked a treat.
Brownlow's and Fisher's – they were chemists too,
And at the other end of town the herbalist looked after you.
White and Sentence sold pianos and music by the sheet,
And Mr Aldwinkle, the chiropodist, worked wonders on the feet.

'Fishy' Hayes and 'Salty' Salt sold wet fish on demand,
Whilst Dickinson & Morris (still there) sold best pork pies in the land.
Richardson's, Bagshaw's and Gills were all very good shops in town,
As were Brenda's and Hammond's, catering for the jacket and the gown.
War Memorial Hospital – I've spent one or two 'holidays' there,
And with competence and compassion was given my fair share.
The view from out the window was very good to see
With friendly bird or squirrel to aid recovery!

'Potty' Hill sold best-quality glass and crockery
And Bowley's shop window displayed eye-catching jewellery.
It was Mr Inkley (I think) who opened first launderette in town,
Mr Pacey, a well-respected gentleman, made business selling papers
for miles around.
But one thing for sure that Melton did not lack,
Which, strange as it seems, was the dog racing track!

Part of River Eye became the lido
With changing booths and diving board, you know.
Who can recall halcyon days spent at 'Bullies Hole' or 'Swan's Nest'
As youngsters, with fishing rod, and learning to swim – the best!
In Melton's park, near to see-saws and swings,
Was a nice paddling pool for toddlers, with their rubber rings.

Can you remember the Labour Office in Nottingham Street?
Plenty of jobs were on offer for whichever your fancy could meet.
Now, when we see all man-made and natural disasters,
To me it seems quite clear
That we live in a beautiful county, so, when you look around you –
Aren't you glad that you live right here?

O. B. C. T.
(Obesity)

When I was born
My parents closely looked at me
"Crikey, by Jove!" they said,
"She must weigh a stone – or even three . . ."
They had to feed me by the bottle,
Milk tankered in – full cream,
They couldn't keep me satisfied,
For more and more I'd scream.

I'd cry for food both day and night
How could parents deal with that?
It seems that I was destined
Even then, for ever to be fat!
At nursery school it used to be law
To provide a third of a pint of full-cream milk
For us to drink with a straw.
"Now stand in line children,
And take your turn."
I'd be drinking mine by the gallon,
Straight from the churn!

Thro' the length of all my schooldays
At sport I was no good,
But I could beat the fastest
To get my meat, two veg and pud!
'Twasn't that I was greedy,
But I was never satisfied, you see,
I just had to have a lot to eat
To boost my energy.

Teenage days should be happy days
But companions can be cruel,
It isn't trendy to be 'pudgy' –
'Slimline' is the rule.
I'd dress up to go dancing
To meet the partner of my dreams,
But I was always thwarted
Of any romantic schemes.
I'd stand there looking wistful,
Hoping my turn to dance would come soon,
Till I heard some fellow saying,
"I ain't a-dancing with that there fat balloon!"

The more depressed I came
The more I ate –
I had to have food to compensate.
Sausages, pies, fish and chips,
I shovelled 'em all between my lips.
Chocolate, cream cakes, puds and jams,
All served to increase the size of my hams.

"Why, oh why?" I'd ask myself,
"Should it be that I've been cussed
By being crossed by an African elephant
And a swarm of all-consuming locust?"

I've made up my mind now,
I'm really going to try
To cut out sugary doughnuts, trifle and pork pie.
I will be slim – you wait and see
I'll definitely start tomorrow . . .
As soon as I've had my tea.

SECOND CHANCE

I've got a bit of a problem –
I know it's rather absurd,
I'll tell you, if you promise me
You won't repeat a word . . .

There's this 'ere chap who fancies me,
He's told me so, you see.
Well, you can see I'm no spring chicken
Yes, I can tell you all agree!
I'll admit I feel quite flattered,
It's certainly a 'second chance',
For a bit of mild flirtation
And a little olde-world romance.

He said, "I think you are lovely,"
By Jove, I felt quite grand,
Just like a beautiful heroine
From the pen of Barbara Cartland.
He tells me when I'm looking good,
But he doesn't always speak that kind
Because he'll tell you outright
Just what's on his mind:
When invited to a wedding I bought a feathered hat,
"You're never going to wear", he said,
"A horrible thing like that!"

Together we've visited places
I haven't seen for years.
I sometimes tell myself,
"It can only end in tears."
But for now I'll take my chance,
It surely can't be wrong,
The fact that every time I see him
My heart is filled with song.

Do you think I should feel guilty
That I've another man –
Or, should happiness be taken
As and when one can?
I bet you think I'm quite a fool
To get involved this way,
But I just can't help my feelings
Whatever folk may say.

I'm a 'crinkly', with spots and dandruff,
But I feel years younger every day.
Anyway, beauty's in the eye of the beholder –
At least that's what they say.

But things are moving far too fast
They're getting out of hand.
I'll have to put my foot down
And make him understand.
He said, "I'd like to marry you."
I said, "Well, blow me down –
I just don't think that's possible,
While Grandad's still in town.
But come now, sit upon my knee."
My lovely little grandson –
At the worldly age of three.

FIT AS A FIDDLE

Well, hello there – if it isn't Florrie Brown,
It's very nice to see you,
I heard you were back in town.
How are you then? You're looking great –
You've kept your figure trim,
How's that handsome husband now
Do I remember that his name was Jim?
You WHAT! – He went and cleared off with WHO?
Oh, I really don't believe what things are coming to!

How am I? Well, I really can't complain,
But I've never been the same
Since I had that Asian flu again.
And my bunions – I don't know how I manage to walk!
And my throat's been oh so dry and sore,
I find it hard to talk!
Oh, the pain from my back when I get to bed at night,
Only us who suffer – know just what it's like!

Mind you, my spots don't seem so bad
Now I'm using that new cream.
Ah! just because I **look** so well
Things are never what they seem.
For instance – these poor legs of mine,
Are knotted up with veins,
And my shoulder blades and neck
Are full of rheumatic pains.

My chest – it's been that bad –
I can hardly breathe, you know,
And I've really cut down on the fags
To about only forty a day or so.
My stomach worries me
It seems to be quite bloated,
And look at my tongue –
You must agree it's really quite fur-coated.

Doctor said to me, "Cut down on the fat",
With him I must agree,
But I only have chips FOUR times a week
I can't see much harm in **that!**
I need a hip replacement
Ah, if you can afford it – it's OK for some.
(But I'll tell you a little secret –
I'm considering liposuction on my bum!)

Well, I can't stand here and gossip
It's all right for some, I suppose,
I'll just pop into the chemist
For something to unblock my nose.
Then I really must dash and nip home now,
Because I have to pick up my kit –
You mean to say you can't tell, dear –
That I'm into aerobics and keep-fit?

LIVING IN THE PAST

I'm finally going to admit it – at last!
I've always been told and now I know – I'm living in the past.
When washer or kettle or similar goes wrong,
"How long have you had it?" is said –
"Only five or six years, it isn't that old."
"Bin it – it's had it, splash out on another instead!"
My mother had a Frigidaire it lasted forty years or so,
But that was long ago, things aren't made to last now, you know.

Under Swan Porch was a butcher's shop, manned by Ben,
It was customary to see a queue on a Saturday morning then.
I was sent with ration books and ten-bob note to buy the weekly treat,
To buy a joint and take home change – only now in dreams could we compete.
Perks' shop used to have a machine that sliced bacon
Into rashers of both thick and thin,
Now bacon comes pre-packed, full of water,
No lovely fat to dip your bread crusts in!

'Twas more friendly to shop back in those days,
And a chair by the counter had space,
And a word and a smile by the server,
Made the shop seem a friendlier place.
With all modern packaging of cling film and cardboard
I really can't quite come to terms –
And with folk a-coughing and sneezing
We built up our own resistance to germs.

When starting work I earned thirty bob a week,
Which bought little bits and pieces and paid for my keep.
Oh, I'm quite well aware that all is relative,
But it really makes me wonder what the future has to give!
When in civil defence they taught me how to drive,
And a gallon of petrol cost two shillings and six old pence.
Now just one postage stamp seems to cost much more –
To me it just doesn't seem to make any sense!

But on the plus side there is no more dolly tub
For clothes to wash and mangle and even give a rub –
Just bung them in the washer and out they come quite clean,
Now sometime in the future no ironing is the dream.
And if you are feeling idle and just don't want to cook,
Put a pre-packed meal in the micro and ignore the cookery book!
I'm beginning to learn the lesson – in the past it's nice to dream,
But I'll stay put in the present cos – like the cat – I've got the cream!
However, having said that I'd like to make it clear,
I'm pleased I was born in my memory days
Of good old yesteryear!

PAST – OR PRESENT?

Tell me, do you ever, the same as me –
Try to visualise Melton as it used to be?
Do your thoughts ever stray
To bygone days – pre Norman Way –
When Melton was a small quaint town
With no traffic lights for miles around?

Norman Way was then Norman Street
With the police station situated there,
Many coppers roamed the beat,
And about security we never thought to care.
Beaver the baker was where Nicko's fish shop now stands,
Oh, I remember their bread, cakes and buns,
Which tasted right grand!

Remember Watchorn's shop, with three brass balls adorned,
With window full of pitiful treasures,
By necessity having been pawned.
Can you remember Assembly Rooms –
Well known for their 'Saturday Hop'?
And just across the road
Was Farrow's pork pie and faggot shop,
Where, at the same time of purchase, as I'm sure you may know,
One could book Farrow's buses to see a first-class show.

In Nottingham Street, hardly spoken about now (quite strange),
Stood the building, as the name implied, 'The Corn Exchange'.
I remember the market place with gaslit stalls,
And Barnes block was there the memory recalls.
There were plenty of good grocer shops there as well:
Melia's, Lipton's, Perks', and of course
Easom's – with its well-remembered coffee smell.

There was a choice of Plaza or Regal for 'flicks'
And after a fish-and-chip supper,
Which foremost in the memory sticks.
And a memory of which you may well share,
Is being served by poor Mrs Haddon
With the 'earphone-style' hair.
Into Brownlow's cycle shop we'd often peek
At bikes you could buy for a tanner a week.
Whilst Humphries' shop sold toffees, sweets and rocks,
And Brotherhood's tempted with the latest fashion in frocks.
Atkinson's cafe was in Burton Street,
As was Sutton's – with bacon and sausages a succulent treat.

Once Melton boasted about thirty pubs – which may amaze,
From King's Head to Black's Head and including the Bishop's Blaze.
I also remember names like Marriot's Stores and the Penny Bazaar,
With shoe shops like Leader's and Rowell's –
To which gentry came from near and afar.

There was Oakley the tailors, Littler the vet and
'Six-Foot' the dwarf who delivered papers,
And I haven't finished yet . . .
There were doctors, Bishop and Manson, and dentist, Arnsby
(Who extracted teeth better when topped up with drink),
But, the best known of local characters was Dolly Pepper,
I would think!

Most of our memories are fading with time,
Could it be that we glossed them to make them sublime?
Did we wear rose-tinted glasses to enhance our view?
I have my thoughts and I guess that you do too . . .
Was Melton best in the past – or is it far better now?
At this point, I'm off – before I begin to incite a row!

WINTER

I HATE winter – I detest the cold –
Must say I didn't notice it
Till I started growing old.
Oh, I know it looks quite pretty,
With frost on hedge and tree,
But it's gale-force winds and rain and sleet
That really exasperate me.

I just cannot stand the cold, you know,
It gets in all my joints,
It penetrates my thermals,
And freezes vital points.
Even trying to get my washing dry
Used to make me scream and shout,
But I've got so's I don't bother now –
I just turns 'em inside out!

I'm really quite a wimp, you know,
When I've caught the dreaded cold,
With streaming eyes and runny nose –
At least that's what I'm told.
I gargle with the Lemsip,
I wear an extra vest,
And I slap on loads of goose grease
Upon my poor old chest.

Ooh, I'm pleased that folk can't see me
When I toddle off to bed,
With bright-pink woolly bedsocks
And a Noddy cap on my head.
Armed with my hot-water bottle,
Snug in duvet – 15 tog –
No wonder bedroom window
Is all steamed up with fog!

Folks say it's healthy
When a winter frost is hard,
But I only like snow and icicles
When they're on a Christmas card.
Yes, wintertime really gets me
In such a depressing state,
I'm looking for warmer places
To which to emigrate.

But even when I moan and groan
I don't mean all I say,
For there's a wonderful compensation
Which brightens up each day –
A real good open fire
Stoked up with logs and coal,
To warm the body thro' and thro'
Unto the very soul.

And when at night you sit and dream,
And into the flames you gaze,
The pictures there before you
Most surely will amaze.
Something else I'll tell you too,
Not many folks can boast,
Of sitting by the fireside
A-making rounds of toast!

Well, I'll admit that wintertime
Holds pleasures too for you,
Like spotted dick and custard
And dumplings and stew.
But I would like to say just one thing,
I can't wait to say, "Goodbye, winter,
And welcome, lovely spring."

LIKE ME

My mother brought me up properly,
I crook my finger whilst drinking tea,
Never from the saucer would I drink
And to burp aloud I dare not even think!
Why, oh why, can't everyone be
A perfect person – just like me?

I'm sure that no one here would ever believe
I'd wipe my nose upon my sleeve,
For a handkerchief I never have to beg,
One is always neatly folded
Up my knicker leg.
Why, oh why, can't everyone be
A perfect person – just like me?

I've never been known to curse or swear
(At least not when I know that anyone's there),
I don't scratch my head – at least not twice –
For folk like me just don't get lice.
Why, oh why, can't everyone be
A perfect person – just like me?

For appointments I am never late,
From the truth I never deviate,
I close my mouth when I eat my food
And to my 'betters' I am never rude.
Why, oh why, can't everyone be
A perfect person – just like me?

I ne'er complain what's put on my plate
If it looks and tastes putrid I'd say that it's great,
You never see me trying to push in in a queue
That sort of thing, only common folk do.
Why, oh why, can't everyone be
A perfect person – just like me?

It's rude to use your fingers
When your teeth you need to pick,
My parents taught me how to use a little stick.
When I've missed a conversation
I wouldn't dream of saying, "What?"
"Pardon me" will adequately display
The manners that I've got.
Why, oh why, can't everyone be
A perfect person – just like me?

I wouldn't eat peas from the back of my fork,
And I'd never indulge in 'dirty talk'.
I've never been known to suck my thumb,
And no one ever catches me a-scratching my bum . . .
Why, oh why, can't everyone be
A perfect person – just like me?

I always say, "Thanks" and "Pretty please",
And turn my head when I have to sneeze.
I cut my toenails in complete privacy
And I'm well known for my utmost modesty.
Why, oh why, can't everyone be
A perfect person – just like me?

I never sweat – just discreetly perspire,
I'm always cautious and don't play with fire.
I can't help being perfect – it must be in the genes,
Everyone's so jealous – or perhaps that's how it seems.
Why, oh why, can't everyone be
A perfect person –just like me?

One thing I haven't mentioned – it may cause some surprise,
The BEST thing that I'm good at
Is telling loads of lies.
Why, oh why, can't everyone be
A perfect FIBBER – JUST LIKE ME!

FRIENDS?

My grandson, Jack, has a cat!
Well, there's nothing unusual about that!
But Boris, for that's his name,
Has quite a special claim to fame.
You see, Boris thinks he's royalty,
He considers he's better than you or me.
He's black and white, quite handsome too,
With big yellow eyes that stare at you.

His fur is sleek and his tail is straight and high,
And he tends to ignore you as he regally walks by.
He doesn't mix with other cats,
Or put himself out to chase mice and rats.
His food he eats quite daintily,
And he washes his ears most regularly.
He likes a tickle under his chin and behind his ear,
But enough is enough he soon makes clear.

A beanbag by the radiator is his daytime bed,
And at night his address is 'No.10 Box' just inside the shed.
Yes, Boris leads the life of a king,
But can I ask you just one thing?
"Why doesn't Boris like Jack Handley's poor old nan?"
I really try to please him, the very best I can,
But each time I walk in through the door,
He eyes me up and sharpens each and every claw.

I try to make friends by tickling his head –
But his tail starts to lash and his eyes go all red!
I won't show I'm scared, so I turn on the charm,
But he scratches my leg and digs his teeth in my arm.
Why can't we be friends, Boris?
I promise not to tease –
Even though your fur gets up my nose
And makes me want to sneeze.

Come, sit on my lap and do not stir,
You luscious little bundle of fur and purr.
Let's make a resolution of friendship – you and me,
Then I can honestly say, "Welcome to the family –
Boris Handl-ey!"